veneziainpiccolo

Giorgio Gianighian
Paola Pavanini

Venice: the basics

Illustrations
Giorgio Del Pedros

GAMBIER&KELLER
editori

conception
Madile Gambier
Giovanni Keller

texts
Giorgio Gianighian
Paola Pavanini

illustrations
Giorgio Del Pedros

graphic design
Peppe Clemente, studio cheste

translation
Christina Cawthra

Sixth edition, September 2015

ISBN: 978-88-96224-26-7

www.gambierkeller.com

Grateful thanks go to Antonio Fancello
for his help and assistance.

The maps of the urban development
on p. 14 and p. 15 are the graphic re-elaborations
from material published in E. Trincanato,
Venise au fil du temps, *Paris 1971.*

We would like to describe the material and physical origins of Venice, which arose from the water like a sort of miracle in stone

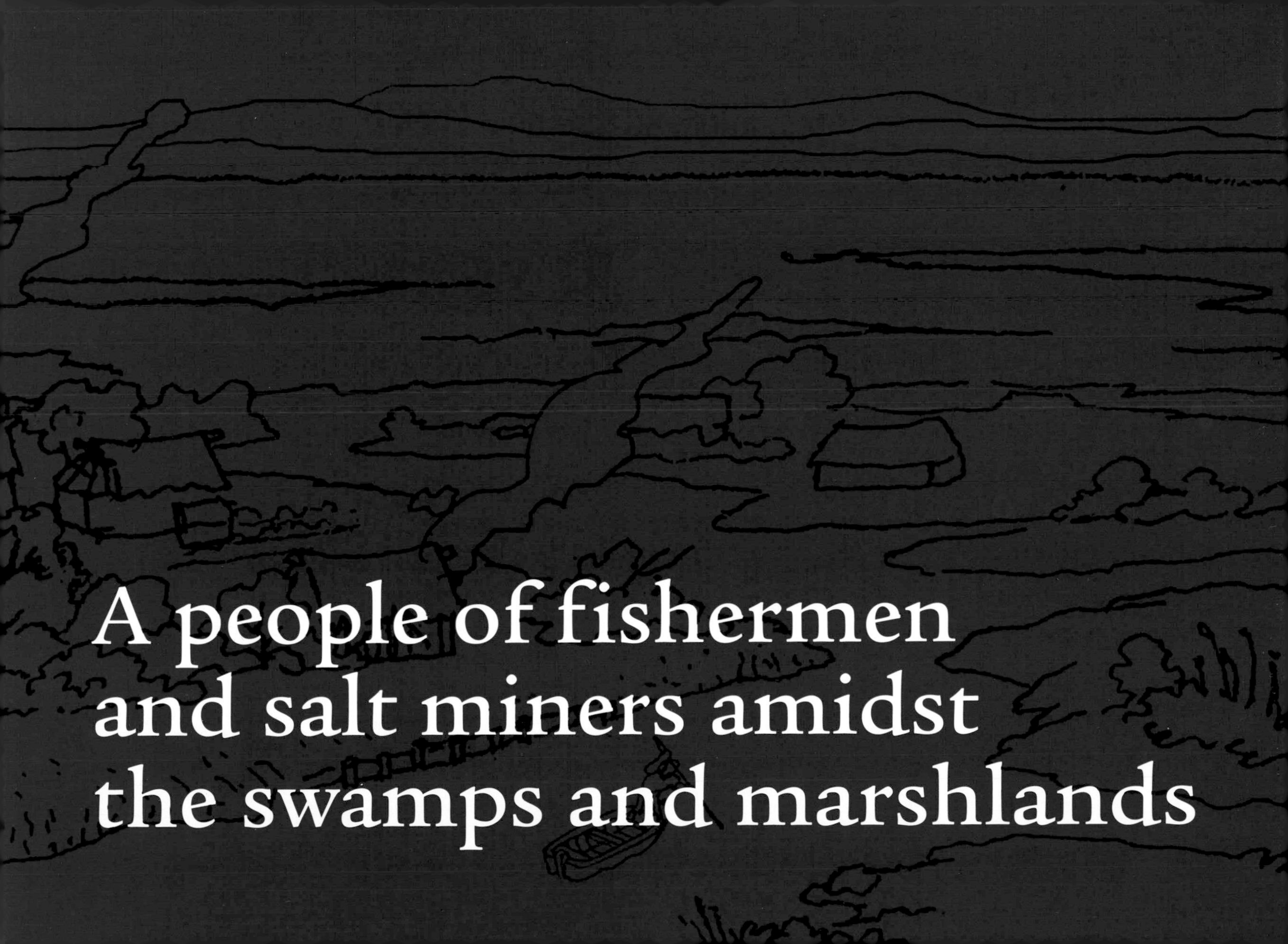

A people of fishermen
and salt miners amidst
the swamps and marshlands

Scholars have discussed the origins of Venice for years, and some even believe it to have Roman roots, surmising later geological changes. However, this is not what we want to talk about: we would like to describe the material and physical origins of Venice, which arose from the water like a sort of miracle in stone.

There is no doubt that this miracle was the result of human effort and intelligence. With unwavering perseverance, the first people who settled in these brackish waters not only built houses but also the land upon which they could build. Thanks to the salt industry, it was the sea water itself that laid the foundations for their future wealth.

Before the lagoon actually became the lagoon of Venice, from the very first centuries of Christianity it was these peoples of fishermen and salt miners who managed to become stronger and richer, thanks both to their own hard work and historically favourable circumstances. The nature surrounding them was cruel and did not appear to offer any possibility for settlement expansion. The only solution was to wrest the land from the water, doing so in two directions: on the one hand, they had to reinforce the land that had surfaced, which was easily submerged by the tides; on the other, they quite literally had to steal their living space from the lagoon.

Thanks to the salt industry, it was the sea water itself that laid the foundations for their future wealth.

It meant encircling the land with a serried row of piles (known as a palisade) and filling the area they had created with materials left over from building sites or debris from elsewhere.

The techniques they used to achieve these results were complex.
It meant encircling the land with a serried row of piles (known as a palisade) and filling the area they had created with materials left over from building sites or debris from elsewhere. This was how they created new, stable terrain that was then pounded to make it stronger.
These tiny reinforced, strengthened islands were obviously created along the banks of canal or on the edges of the lagoon. The reinforcement of the boundary between the land and water with rows of piles and embankment walls, creating the characteristic pedestrian quays we call *fondamente*, had a two-fold purpose: to allow pedestrian circulation and to stop the tides eating away what had been taken from the sea with such effort.
Much later on, over the centuries the main areas of the city were paved with bricks, as was the case in all Italian cities in the Middle Ages. It was not until much later that the stone paving we can see today was laid.

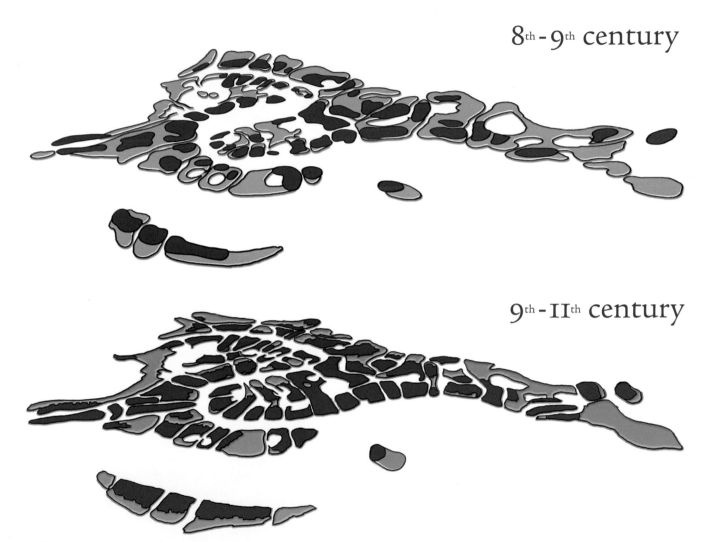

8th-9th century

9th-11th century

It is obvious that this process of reinforcement
and expansion was both long and laborious.
Around 1000, Venice was a small city with
numerous 'pools' or 'lakes' dotted about,
containing very few streets and bridges
but made up of numerous islands.

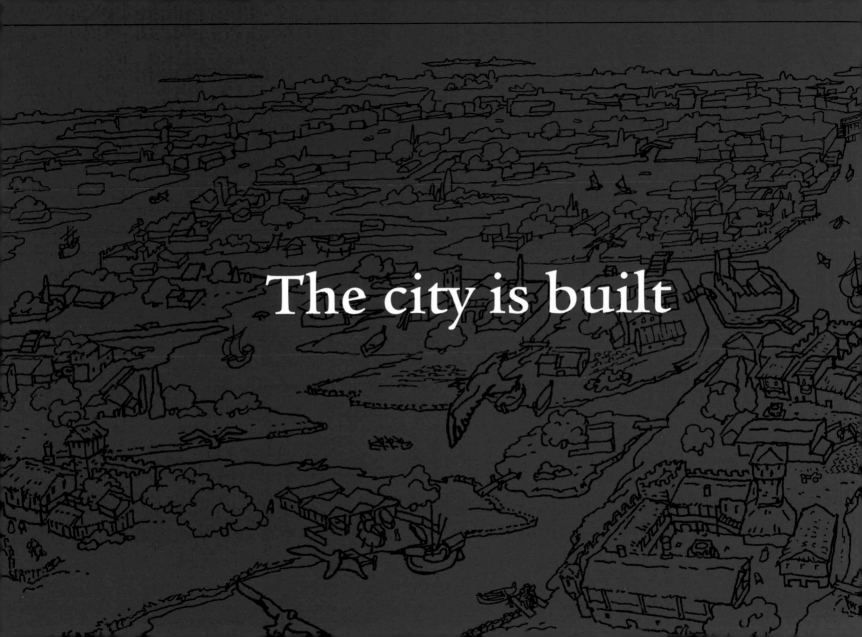

The city is built

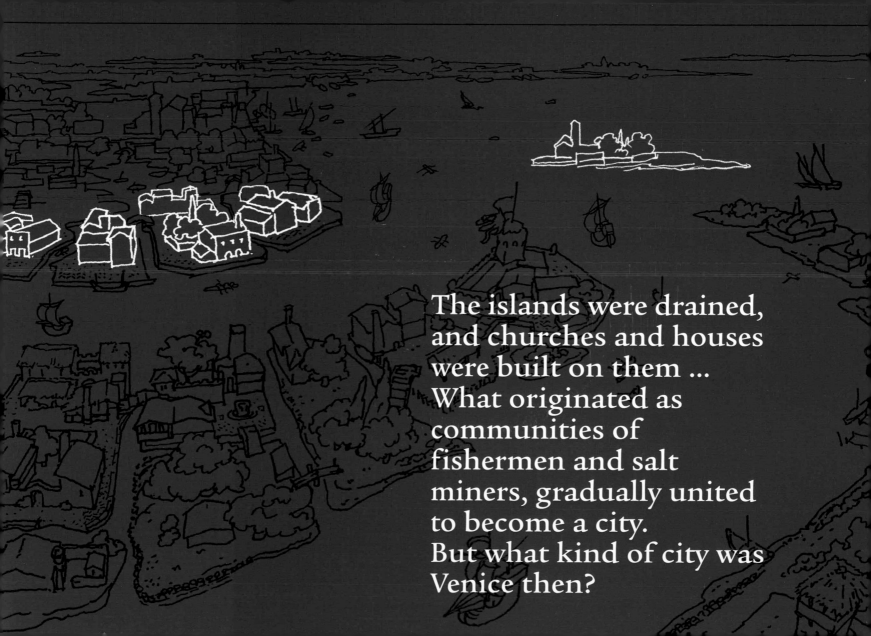

The islands were drained,
and churches and houses
were built on them ...
What originated as
communities of
fishermen and salt
miners, gradually united
to become a city.
But what kind of city was
Venice then?

The islands were drained, and churches and houses were built on them ... *Palazzi,* or perhaps castles for the more powerful, humble abodes for the common people. What originated as communities of fishermen and salt miners gradually united to become a city. By sometime around the year 1000 the settlement in the hostile lagoon had become worthy of the name 'city'. But what kind of city was Venice then?

There were certainly a lot of churches, most of which were still in wood (although the most central Church of San Salvador still had a thatched roof in 1365), and there were also lots of convents: many of the place names we still use today for our streets and squares (called *campi* in Venice) are derived from parishes and convents. Every time a new piece of land was drained, a church would be built there to take care of the spiritual health of the settlement.

There was a Doge's palace, perhaps still in wood or mostly in wood, which burnt down in 976 together with the Church of Saint Mark and numerous houses, when the Venetians set fire to them in protest against the Doge. And the houses? These would have been more like fortified castles than *palazzi,* and each one was surrounded by the homes of the common people who depended on the noble family. This was a feudal relationship, where the powerful would protect those who laboured on their land, and they in turn would serve their masters. These castles were often in conflict with one another and there was therefore no great need for roads of communication, other than those required to reach the church or Doge's Palace. They would move around on the waterways, using the boats the inhabitants tied to their houses – like pets, as an ancient chronicler once wrote in amazement.

Most of the 'pools' inside the built up area had been drained and there were no longer enough waterways: commerce established itself and the various islands would constantly trade with each other.

The families' interests gradually gave way to the central power of the Doge and the inhabitants began to be defined on the basis of which parish they belonged to: by the tenth and eleventh centuries, there were already around sixty parishes.

Most of the 'pools' [*piscine* in Venetian] inside the built up area had been drained and there were no longer enough waterways: commerce established itself and the various islands would constantly trade with each other. Overland links became necessary: *calli* [alleys], *fondamente* [waterside streets], *rughe* [commercial streets] and bridges above all, to cross the countless canals surrounding the islands.

It was not until much later (twelfth-thirteenth century) that the streets, *calli,* were named after the *palazzi* or church they led to (as well as their function), when both the water and street network became public, having originally been mainly private.

Streets or quayside streets (*riva*) and squares (*campi*) were made of beaten earth but it was not long before the entire network was paved, starting from the Merceria, first using herring-bone bricks, and then later, in the seventeenth century, with the slabs (*masegni*) we can still see today. These are large rectangular stones (ashlars) of Euganean trachyte, smoothed on only the side that is walked upon.

The sides of the canals [*rio* in Venetian] were reinforced with a foundation made of piles driven deep into the water, with a raft [*zatterone* in Venetian] made of large planks of wood nailed to it; a brick wall was then built on it, thus creating a permanent, effective separation between the land and the water. Blocks of Istrian stone were then placed on it, often with rings attached to tie up the boats when goods were being loaded and unloaded.

beaten earth

herring-bone bricks

masegni
slabs of Euganean trachyte

blocks of Istrian stone

brick wall

brick wall

zatterone
raft made of planks of wood

piles driven into the water

While talking about bridges – over the ages no fewer than 450 (plus one) have been built, both public and private (in fact, just under one hundred lead exclusively to a house), culminating in the new link between Piazzale Roma (the terminal for cars and buses) and the Railway Station. But in the past? The first constructions used to cross the canals were probably just simple walkways made of wood, put down when needed, and removed immediately afterwards so the water traffic could continue unhindered. They gradually became permanent, with the addition of steps, making it possible to cross the canal, but were still made of wood, with permanent piles and planks. Lots of these can be seen on ancient maps. However, wood and salt water do not always agree, and these wooden bridges required constant repairs and maintenance. From the fourteenth century onwards, if not earlier, they were therefore replaced by bridges made of brick and stone. Only one bridge crossed the Grand Canal, the Rialto Bridge, and that was also made of wood until the end of the sixteenth century when it was replaced by the one we can still see today. Numerous *traghetti* (the gondola crossings you can still see today) were used to cross the Grand Canal and it was not until the second half of the eighteenth century that a second bridge was built. This was a sort of iron walkway between the Accademia and San Vidal; it was later replaced by a wooden bridge that has recently been reinforced.

The Scalzi Bridge, which links Santa Croce and the Railway Station, was also originally made of iron before it was rebuilt in the twentieth century. Finally, there is the bold and extremely modern fourth bridge across the Grand Canal, which has just been inaugurated, and has been baptised "Calatrava Bridge".

The first constructions were just simple mobile walkways made of wood. Over the years they became permanent, with the addition of steps so they crossed the canal.

The nobility would travel around by gondola, food products were transported from the mainland in a *caorlina*, while the *peate* transported bricks, timber and anything else needed for construction.

Let us go back to the canals that still play a key role in transport, of goods in particular, but that have always played a much more important role in getting around the city than the streets. It was in a gondola that the nobility travelled to run their errands, in gondolas the ladies would go from one house to another; in *caorlinas* (a boat used for transportation) food products would be transported from the mainland and the islands; while *burchi* and *peate* (large barges) transported bricks, timber and anything else needed for construction, and it was only by boat that one could reach the city: water was therefore the heart and life of Venice, source of all wealth and defence against the enemies. Hence, in the grand patrician *palazzi*, the main entrance was not from the street, often some dark little alleyway, but from the water.

27

The lagoon was also a better form of protection than any kind of city wall or fortifications system: when the Genoese laid siege to Venice in 1379, occupying part of the lagoon and Chioggia, the island system around the city was fortified and the fleet expanded. Until the French arrived at the end of the eighteenth century, this was the only occasion that the Venetian Republic risked occupation, and it was the lagoon that saved her. In turn, over the centuries the government did their utmost to ensure that work was carried out on the waterways and rivers to preserve the city and protect it from silting.

However, the salt water had another essential but humble task: cleaning the city. The entire sewerage system in Venice is entrusted to the canals that take away the dirty water and replace it with clean sea water twice a day: "l'aqua va in mar" and "il mar va in aqua" ['the water goes out to sea' and 'the sea goes to water'] is how the Venetians describe this process. Today the sea might not be as clear as it once was, but the rising tide still brings a flood of clean water into every canal in the city, taking away all kinds of filth. This was why Venice was considered a clean, healthy city, at least until new technology equipped the other cities with more modern, efficient sewage systems. Indeed, without exception all houses had a ceramic plumbing system inside the walls, called *canoni da necessario* (the meaning of *necessario* – indispensable – should be clear) that would empty the waste into the *gatoli,* the canalization system under the street pavement. From there it went into the canals.

Today this is basically how it still works, although several additional precautions are taken: before the waste reaches the canals, it is deposited and filtered in biological tanks although other hygienic measures are

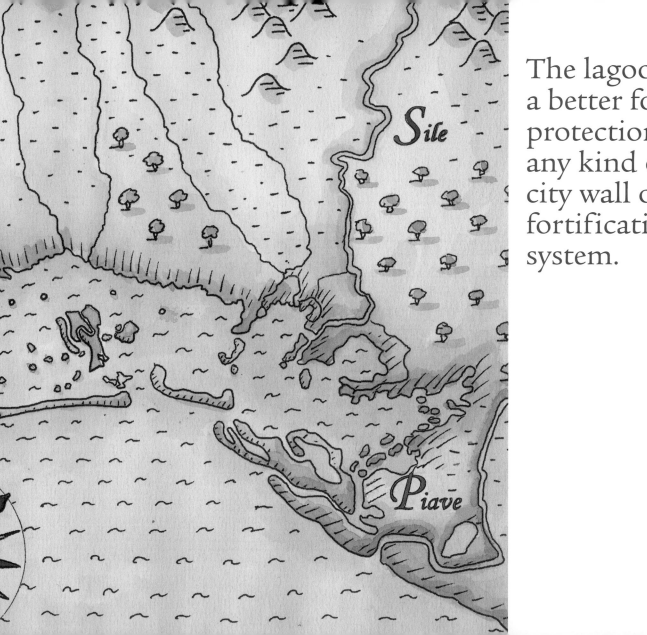

The lagoon was
a better form of
protection than
any kind of
city wall or
fortifications
system.

taken for hotels and other community residences. However, the tides still play a key role in city hygiene.

"Water, water everywhere, ... nor any drop to drink": but how did the city quench its thirst?

When you are walking around Venice, even if you are distracted, you cannot help but notice that in every *campo,* in every courtyard, wherever there is a little space outdoors, there is a beautiful stone structure, varying in sizes and decoration, at times bearing patrician coats of arms, at other with figures. They all look very similar to the ones that are called wells on the mainland: a hole in the ground dug deep enough to reach the aquifer to draw water. And that is what the Venetians call them – wells – but they aren't wells at all. There is no freshwater to be had in the subsoil of the city, only brackish water which is of little use for domestic purposes: "Venice is in the water and has no water", they used to say every time their attempts to find an aquifer or source were of no avail. They found something on the Lido, but it was not much, and even less in the city. The 'wells' were therefore cisterns that collected and conserved invaluable rainwater. When that was not enough, the water was transported by boat-tankers from the mainland. However, these cisterns also had to take into account the problem of the clayey, salty Venetian subsoil; they not only had to devise a system to isolate the contents but also to find an effective way of collecting the rainwater. The rooftops were the first basin: rainwater would fall from the overhanging pitches on the streets (and the passers-by), where it was collected and funnelled into the cisterns. Later (in the fourteenth century) the roof pitches were constructed in line with the façades

"Water, water everywhere, ... nor any drop to drink": but how did the city quench its thirst?

and had stone gutters (*gorne*) that would channel the water without disturbing people passing below, and from there it would go to the cisterns.

The cistern was constructed as follows: a hole that was around 3.5 metres deep would be dug, the size of which depended on the size of the area outdoors. The hole was then lined with clay to waterproof it and a thick round stone slab was placed in the centre; the circular pipe of the cistern rested on this and was made with special bricks that were roundish in shape and called *pozzali*. When it reached the pavement the pipe was crowned by a well-head, usually in Istrian stone. The hole was filled with sand which acted as a filter. In the upper part a sort of brick gallery was built, called a *cassone,* where most of the rainwater was collected via the so-called *pilelle,* stone slabs with several holes, placed in the four corners of the paving around the cistern, either in brick or stone, from where it would then be channelled down to fill the caisson. It trickled down slowly through the filter, or sponge, depositing any impurities on the way. The well was closed with an iron cover that was sometimes locked.

This system required an outdoor area where the water could be channelled from the rooftops and the pavements. We can see a detailed picture of Venice at the end of the Middle Ages in the view by Jacopo de' Barbari, published in 1500: there are many uncovered areas dotted around the city, many more than in other contemporary Italian cities. Thus, this vital necessity of life, the conservation of something as precious as water, resulted in a particular urban form.

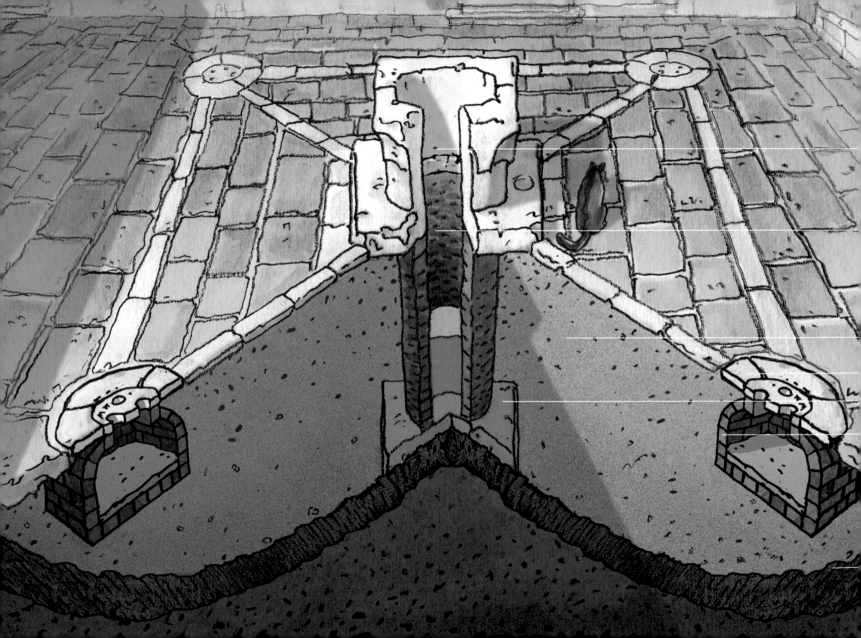

well-head

circular pipe made with
special bricks (*pozzali*)

spongia sand filter

pilella stone slabs with holes

stone slab

cassone brick gallery

waterproof clay

However, one must remember that the rainwater did not always meet all the city's needs and extra water often had to be found.

In such cases large barges, called *burchi,* would load water on the mainland and bring it to Venice, where it was distributed in the cisterns.

People selling water could also be seen on the streets. To simplify and speed up this additional water supply, in 1611 the government approved the construction of a canal, the Seriola, that channelled the water of the River Brenta to the edge of the city so that the barges did not have to travel so far.

It is worth looking at a few figures. The amount of water available per person in the sixteenth century was around 5-5.5 litres a day; two hundred years later, the figure had risen to 6.8. Today, the aqueduct brings around 300-350 litres a day per person – it is impossible to go backwards and nobody even wants to, but maybe we should cut back a little ...!

This system was both ingenious and highly functional, but it required vast open spaces, something that was in direct contradiction to the permanent lack of building land that characterised the growth of the city. A little later on we shall describe how the Venetians managed to reconcile the collection of water with the saving of land, as a result of the demographic growth at the end of the fifteenth century.

At the end of the fifteenth century Venice
was nearly completely built of stone, all of its spaces
were well-defined, its land was drained, and water
was clearly regulated almost everywhere

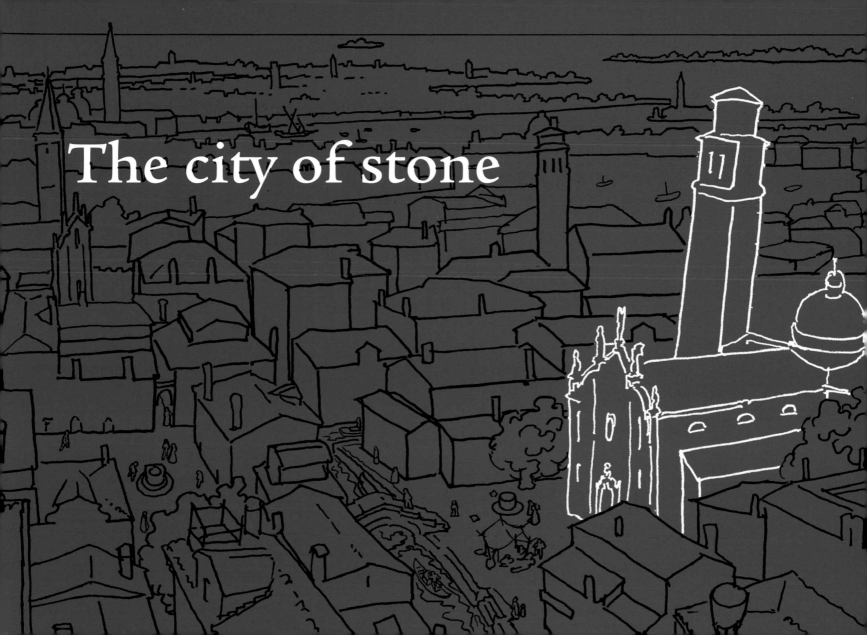

The city of stone

It was in the year 1500 that a 'bird's eye view' of Venice was printed, a woodcut by Jacopo de' Barbari that is still the basis for all studies of the urban structure of the city and its individual buildings today. It was not the first map and it was certainly not the last. Just like every other large city, throughout its history Venice was the subject of countless maps, views, perspectives, panoramas, whether partial or complete, picturesque or realistic... Over eighty were published by scholars, from which innumerable copies were derived. However, this one was a milestone, owing to both its beauty and accuracy and gives us a definite image of the city at the end of the fifteenth century: a city that was completely made of stone by that period, one in which all the spaces were well-defined, land drained and the waterways well-regulated almost everywhere. There were very few areas on the edges that had not yet been used, but as a whole, the city was complete. We can clearly see the squares and courtyards with their cisterns; the churches with their bell towers; and the *palazzi*, houses, both small and large, are all clearly visible. The vast area occupied by the Arsenale stands out immediately – the State ship building yard with its basins, quays and warehouses.

What is the most surprising is just how much has been preserved in the city: if you compare this map to a present-day one, you would think that hardly a day has gone by. The shape is the same, the islands and islets in the lagoon are the same, and the southern side on the water is almost the same. Of course there are differences, and considerable ones at that, in particular on the western border where bridges and terminals for the railway station and cars have united Venice with the rest of the world.

At the beginning of the sixteenth century the city was already unified and highly organised: streets, squares, bridges and canals – everything in place and built to perfection.

However, the city has preserved many of its earlier characteristics: it is crisscrossed by streets and waterways, and the Grand Canal in particular runs through the city exactly as it used to, separating the districts on the one side from those on the other with its outstanding, uninterrupted row of *palazzi*. Venice has always been divided into six districts (called *sestieri* in Italian), three on the one side of the Canal and three on the other. On this side (*de Citra*), i.e. on the side of Saint Mark's Square, we have the *sestieri* of San Marco, Castello and Cannaregio. On the other (*de Ultra*), i.e. across the Rialto Bridge, we have the smaller ones of San Polo, Dorsoduro and Santa Croce.

This division is important because it forms the basis of the house numbering system and is, in fact, slightly bizarre: each *sestiere* starts with 1 and continues to the last house along winding, unforeseeable routes. An additional problem is that certain place names are repeated, making it extremely difficult at times to find an address. Calle della Malvasia 3341 is impossible to find if you do not know which *sestiere* it is in (and even if you do ...) This makes Venice a city in which even the most knowledgeable lose their way. But losing your way in Venice is a pleasure, as long as you are not in a hurry and have time to look around.

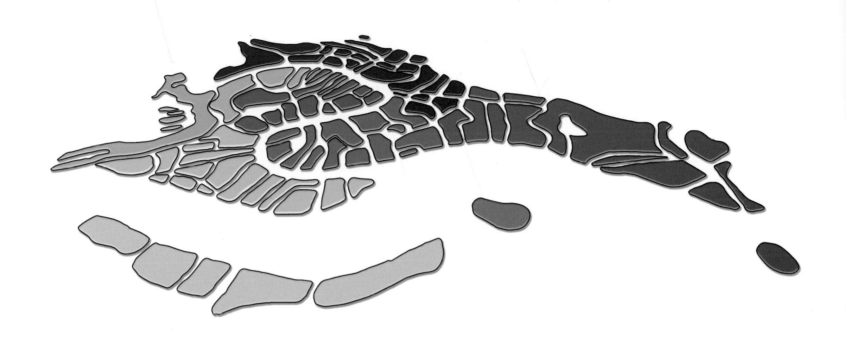

 Dorsoduro   Santa Croce   San Polo   Cannaregio   San Marco   Castello

de Ultra   *de Citra*

Venice has always been divided into *sestieri*, three on the one side of the Saint Mark's Square (*de Citra*): San Marco, Castello and Cannaregio; and three across the Rialto Bridge (*de Ultra*): San Polo, Dorsoduro and Santa Croce.

With a few slight exceptions on the borders, at the beginning of the sixteenth century the city was already unified and highly organised: streets, squares, bridges and canals – everything had found its place and how it should best be built. But the true heart of any city is its houses, whether private or public. And what are the Venetian houses like? How were they built and how can those stone *palazzi* stand on something as treacherous as clay. How can they have been there for hundreds of years without seeming to suffer from the passing of time? To answer this question, which arises quite naturally to any observer, we have to look at the houses and *palazzi* a little more closely.

First of all, some of them are built directly in the water (you only have to look at all the magnificent *palazzi* along the Grand Canal) while others stand on the ground, which is stable to varying degrees.

The problem is simpler for the latter: once the swampy land has been reinforced, they are built in a similar manner to those on the mainland. But on the water? Obviously these majestic, heavy buildings are not floating in the water as some might want to believe (or dream); no, along the canals or in the lagoon, they are also resting, and how they rest! Their feet are on the ground, and they stand on foundations that are at once mighty and hidden.

These majestic, heavy buildings are not floating on the water but are resting on the ground, on foundations that are both mighty and hidden.

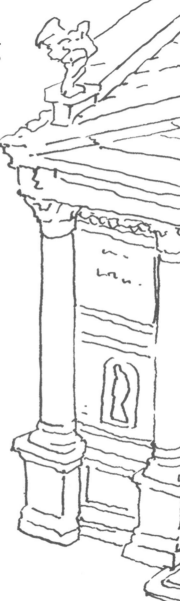

Let us look at what the terrain that supports the city is actually made of. First of all, it is not perfectly horizontal but is wavy, as if it were made up of small hills, in which the centre is denser and has more resistance to the load, which decreases along the borders. By its very nature, its carrying capacity is very low. So the foundations of the heavier (i.e. the taller) buildings had to be dug deep into the ground, where the layers are more compact.

It was not easy to dig deep down in Venice because after just a few shovelfuls, the lagoon water would appear. Nevertheless, dig they had to and dig they did, with the water lapping at their feet, until they reached more solid terrain. Depending on the weight of the building that was to be constructed, they either stopped there or had to continue. The gullet was large, ranging from a minimum of a metre and a half to a maximum of around three metres forty, and its depth depended not only on the weight but also on the precise location of the spot of land. It would be less deep towards the higher part of the 'hill', deeper where it was lower, reaching its maximum in the water where the ground was the least stable. In these cases it had to be reinforced, using techniques similiar to those used along the embankments, by driving

long, two- or three-metre piles into the ground, one next
to the other, and graded towards the top. This is where they then built
the base of the foundations, either nailing a double layer of crossed
larch wood planks to the top of the piles or laying them directly
on the ground; these protruded by around 15-20 centimetres from
the brick foundations (foundation plinth) resting on them.
The name of this boarding – *zatterone* – says it all: a raft, it was called,
giving the idea of something that kept the building afloat on the water.
The plinth foundations had a broad base that gradually decreased
towards the top so that it was of the same thickness as the brickwork
on the ground floor; this great work ended with a series of blocks of
Istrian stone that were placed on the bricks and kept the entire
foundations system together, protecting the brickwork of the building
above from rising damp.
An immense task, regarding both the amount of materials and work:
one only needs to bear in mind that just one linear metre of foundation
required up to four cubic metres of brickwork in the larger buildings.
It is precisely these difficulties and the extremely high cost of the
foundations that explains the extraordinary continuity in the building
fabric of the city: when a building was in ruins or considered too old,
the ancient foundations would be preserved and it was on these that
they worked. More frequently, the 'skeleton' of the building was
preserved, i.e. the bearing structure, and only the façades would be
modified, adapting them to new architectural styles.
Whether great patrician *palazzi* or simple middle-class homes, on such
foundations the buildings built on the water remain remarkably robust.

blocks of Istrian stone

brick foundation plinth

zatterone
raft made of planks of wood

piles driven into the water

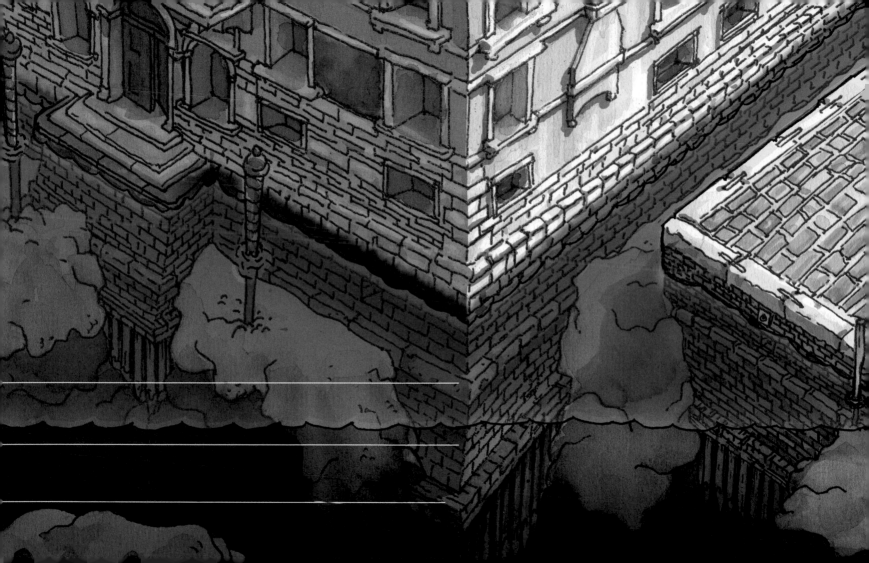

Vigilant visitors will notice that it is not always easy to distinguish a *palazzo* from a 'block of houses' with a number of homes for the 'lower' classes, i.e. tradesmen and professionals.

The *palazzo*, which is called "Casa da stazio" in Venetian, abbreviated in Ca', since the name '*palazzo*' was only used for the Doge's home, is usually made up of one or two homes above one another, usually used by a family's children. This is why there are usually two *piani nobili* above one another (these are the floors with the highest ceilings and usually the most lavishly decorated).

An example will make it clearer. Ca' Gussoni between the Grand Canal and Rio di Noale was built between 1548 and 1556. If we look at the main façade overlooking the Grand Canal we can see it is divided into three: the ground floor with a mezzanine above, two *piani nobili* above that, which are not exactly identical, and then a beautiful central four-light window and balcony. There are two water entrances, an essential feature of every "Ca' da stazio": one on the Grand Canal, the other along Rio di Noale, thus confirming that there were two homes in the building, one on each *piano nobile*.

As always, the side façade is much more modest, but since the rio is quite wide and the façade is visible, it had been adorned with openings with Istrian stone decorations that are connected to one another with a fascia in the same material.

According to ancient sources, the building was designed by Michele Sanmicheli, who also designed other Venetian *palazzi* such as the impressive Ca' Grimani in San Luca (today the Court of Appeal). It was built by Marco Gussoni for himself and his two children and had

The two *piani nobili* had separate staircases and entrances while the layout of the rooms was identical.

one particularly important feature: the façade was richly decorated with frescoes by Jacopo Tintoretto and there were other less important frescoes in the courtyard. This taste for frescoes was particularly widespread in Venice, in particular before the Renaissance, although not only: Fondaco dei Tedeschi – overlooking the Grand Canal next to Rialto Bridge – was built in the early sixteenth century and the main façade was entirely covered with frescoes by Giorgione while those on the side façade were by Titian.

Today the entrance to the *palazzo* is through a small public courtyard at the back, but its main entrance was obviously the one from the water. In the small courtyard we can see a cistern and two staircases, one for each of the *piano nobile*: indeed, the Venetians did not like (and still don't) sharing their staircases or entrances with other neighbours. The result was architectural acrobatics so that each home had its own entrance and staircase. The two apartments shared both the numerous rooms on the ground floor and mezzanine and the large attic. Let us now go up to the *piano nobile*, via the large staircase that takes us straight into the large central hall, called *portego* and illuminated by a large four-light window looking onto the canal, also offering a view of the courtyard. On the sides of this hall we can see the rooms and the kitchen. The layout was extremely simple, and is the same in both *palazzi* and more humble homes, albeit in smaller dimensions. The same arrangement is repeated on the second *piano nobile*, which we reach via a second staircase; while the two homes share the mezzanine. Every *palazzo* has this floor as do most houses in the city and at times there are two: and here we are – there is also a mezzanine in the attic.

The owners usually used mezzanines on the first floor as their business premises.

The owner generally used the mezzanines on the first floor for business and this was also where the lackeys and employees would often sleep. As a result, in Venetian the word *"mezà"* was a synonym for an office while the mezzanines in the attic were used for the servants.

The houses we today call middle-class have a very similar layout. What is interesting, is that from the outside a *palazzo* and a building that is made up of several houses and usually built so it can be let, look remarkably similar: two *piani nobili* of the same height, one or two mezzanines, round arch multiple-light windows that can also be in pairs and are placed so they frame the fireplace, which is not visible and used to heat the rooms around the entrance hall. It is only on the ground floor that one can see numerous entrances and there is not always an entrance from the canal. In actual fact, in certain cases the multiple-light windows are fake in a way: they are the combination of the two-light or three-light windows of the entrance hall and the windows of the adjacent rooms, thus creating a broader, more 'noble' series of openings. At times, these buildings were also frescoed, just like the *palazzi*: for example the main façade of the great building called Castelforte San Rocco in San Polo, where there used to be four spacious, lavish apartments (500 m²) that were usually let to merchants or entrepreneurs, was covered in frescoes that were still clearly visible in the mid-nineteenth century.

The surprises began once you went in: there was one entrance for each home, with its own staircase. Each *piano nobile* was divided into one or two areas, depending on the number of apartments while the mezzanines were divided equally between all the apartments.

Each house was therefore roughly the same size as the others, and had

A complex system of crisscrossing staircases made it possible to have separate entrances.

its own entrance and independent staircase. To make this possible, Venetian architects devised a complex system of crisscrossing staircases that is easier to illustrate than describe. Furthermore, there was a cistern, or more frequently half a cistern in each entrance on the ground floor: they were built into the wall that divided the two entrances so it could be used by the two apartments. This was also an ingenious way to save money since it cost an awful lot to build a cistern and in this way only half as many were needed. The true saving, however, which resulted from the invention of an internal cistern, was being able to construct a building with a water supply that occupied the entire surface area, without having to have a courtyard. A staircase led from the entrance to the first or second floor, and one went directly into the entrance hall that, in the wealthier houses, went from one end of the house to the other and therefore had a façade on each side.

Although the furnishings in houses and *palazzi* also differed, regarding both quantity and quality, they were basically quite similar, as is also the case today: kitchen tools and crockery, boxes and chests for clothes and the household linen (the first wardrobes did not appear until the eighteenth century), chairs and tables, mattresses on various supports, and so on. The decorations were fundamental: a frequent element was 'cordovan', i.e. fine-grained gilded leather that would be hung on the walls, at times covering the entire rooms, examples of which can be seen in the Doge's Palace. There were nearly always paintings, with both religious and profane subjects; some also had sculptures. And the heating? The ceilings were over four metres high, and the rooms large. It must have been freezing! They had fireplaces in the rooms and the

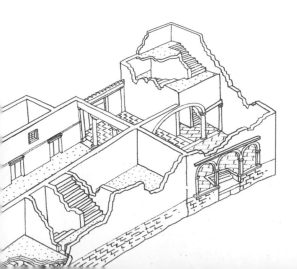

hearth in the kitchen. Something we might find strange is that there were no fireplaces in the entrance hall. They must have had few guests in the winter, since this is where they would be received, or the guests did not stay long … In actual fact, fireplaces were usually placed along the outer walls of the building so that the flues would not have to pass the wooden ceilings and thus pose a fire hazard, a risk that was always lurking. While on the subject, the chimneys themselves also deserve a brief mention because they are both highly visible and characteristic.

The most picturesque are the so-called "bell-shaped" ones that we can see in many Venetian paintings, for example those by Carpaccio.

The buildings in Venice were very close to each other and very often the atmospheric pressure was very low: the combination of these two factors made the uptake of the chimneys very difficult, thus favouring fires, and it was therefore essential that every possible precaution was taken, starting with the chimney for one. It became a highly complex structure: the flue ended in a brick cage that emitted the smoke; this was protected by a sort of shirt (called a *cloak*), that stopped the wind from spreading the sparks as well as helping the uptake by making the most of the cold air meeting the hot smoke .

There is another fundamental difference between the houses and *palazzi* that you can see if you look more closely: a much greater amount of stone was used for the latter, both for the decorations (arches, door and window jambs, façade cladding) and structure (the walls were much thicker). The reason for this is obvious: stone was much more expensive than simple brick, so the greater the quantity, the higher the cost of the building.

52

brick cage

mantello cloak

gorna gutter

We have already seen how these houses and *palazzi* got their supply
of drinking water. But what about the toilet facilities? We have already
mentioned the *gatoli*, the canalisation system under the pavements.
It suffices to say that in the kitchens there was a brickwork cube with
a stone or wooden cover, *necessario*, and this is where the inhabitants
would empty the containers they used or where they would sit.
This was connected to the plumbing, and from here the contents would
flow first into the canalisation system, and then into the canals
or lagoon.
We have already mentioned how a different plumbing system worked
inside the walls: the one that brought rainwater from the roof to the
cistern. We already know about the cistern, and we have also seen
that it required vast outdoor areas. As the population grew and the
building areas had to be exploited to the utmost, the problem was
solved by placing these cisterns inside the houses; they therefore created
a pipe system in the walls that brought the rainwater from the roof
of the building to the cistern(s) on the ground floor.

gorna gutter

canoni da acqua water pipes

necessario latrine

canoni da necessario
sewage pipes

gatolo
underground canalisation system

Houses and *palazzi* for the rich and wealthy – but what about the poor? We know all too well that the greatest part of the population was made up of manual workers, humble craftsmen, sailors, and small-time traders who lived in poverty and could certainly not afford to live in the spacious houses we described earlier. Their houses were simply miniature versions: smaller, but with similar characteristics, starting with the plumbing, and ending with their own entrance. What were different, however, were the houses for those – and there were many – who could not even afford to pay a minimum rent although they were not actually beggars or vagabonds. Countless measures were foreseen for these "deserving poor", and at the top of the list was that they should have a house. Numerous organisations, both public and private, dealt with this matter and many houses were allocated for free (*amore dei*), built in the peripheral areas of the city. These houses were usually built around a courtyard and had two stories. The small apartments consisted in a room and kitchen with fireplace. The cistern was for all the inhabitants and was in the centre of the courtyard. To have an idea of the number of houses that were given to the needy for free for various reasons, we just have to remember that the *Scuole Grandi* (these were guilds of lay confraternities, not schools as we understand them today) allocated at least two hundred houses if not more in the sixteenth century. In addition to these were those of the Procurators of Saint Mark and other small charitable institutions.

Some of these complexes still exist today although they have been modified and additional floors added. If you are interested, you can see an important example that has survived almost unchanged in the area

Two-storey houses for the poor with a central courtyard in the centre with a common well.

of Dorsoduro, not far from Piazzale Roma: *Corte San Marco*, which was named after the *Scuola* that had it built; it used to house 24 apartments, which were twice as large as the usual houses for the needy, in accordance with the wishes of the benefactor who commissioned its construction in his will.

There were a few other groups of houses for charity that did not respect this simple arrangement: perfect examples of these are the houses that are still called of the "Marinarezza" along *Riva degli Schiavoni*. These were arranged in three large buildings that were connected by an arch and were built as homes for sailors from the state fleet who were invalids or too old to work.

The sixteenth century city was therefore basically complete: the urban structure we can see in Jacopo de' Barbari's woodcut is not very different from present-day Venice, with the obvious exception of its links with the mainland. He shows us a dense network of buildings that are interspersed with a large number of open areas that have various functions. First and foremost, the squares, which are usually public areas, with a church towering over them. This is where the social life of the neighbourhood would take place; some used the area for work, at times taking up too much space so the "Giudici del Piovego", magistrates in charge of public urban space, would be forced to intervene. The primary function of these squares, however, as mentioned earlier, was to collect the valuable rainwater, as we can see in the well-heads that almost unfailingly adorn them. Then there were courtyards, both public and private, which usually had a cistern in the

The sixteenth century city was therefore basically complete: the urban structure is not very different from present-day Venice.

centre but at times were also a necessary source of ventilation for the densely built houses around them. These courtyards were certainly the heart of everyday public life: the washing hanging out to dry, women gossiping, children and even adults playing, if the numerous rulings forbidding ball games and dancing are anything to go by, in particular in the courtyards in the poorer quarters, or regarding a series of crimes such as fights and violence of any kind. These repeated, threatening rulings lead one to believe that at night life in the city was not all that peaceful, something that has been confirmed by other sources.

And the gardens: in Venice all too often the gardens are forgotten, regarded as something of little significance while in actual fact, there were a large number. There were the gardens of the nobility, botanical gardens, which the city became famous for, the gardens in convents and cloisters where medicinal herbs were grown. There were vast fruit and vegetable gardens on the Giudecca, not to mention those on the small islands around the city, most of which were occupied by convents that cultivated their own vegetables and gardens. Some of the larger islands (Sant'Erasmo, Vignole) are still important today thanks to their cultivations of excellent garden products.
Today many of these gardens still exist in the city, and are often hidden behind high walls or enclosed between the buildings and almost invisible from outside. It was therefore not only a city of stone, but also a city of green, full of trees, fruit and flowers; it was not until much later that public green areas were to be introduced.

However, these open spaces had another, fundamental function: they were the site of much of the city's industrial activity. We must not forget that Venice was a large manufacturing centre: the wool industry above all, glass and many other minor activities. If the activities were considered dangerous or unhealthy, for example the glass furnaces and tanneries, they were soon sent out of the city and relegated to the surrounding islands (this is why the glass furnaces are still on Murano today), while the others were allowed to remain in different areas in the city. The street names are the best reminder of all the industrial activities in Venice: large rafts made of tree trunks from the Cadore, with all different kinds of timber (planks, boards, strips) from the sawmills would be transported down the mainland rivers and arrive in the city in the north of the lagoon. There were numerous sites for the storage and working of timber in this area, as you can see from the street name that runs parallel to the *Fondamente Nuove*: it is still called *Barbaria delle Tole* (*tole*=tavole= plank). The names *Campo della Lana* ['lana' is Italian for wool], *Fondamenta dei Garzoti, Ramo, Calle etc. delle Chiovere* and *delle Chioverette* are all testimony to the weaving and production of wool in the city. The *chiovere* were an essential feature in the wool industry: this was where the dyed fabric would be laid out to dry and therefore required quite large spaces. In the early 1900s many social houses were built in these areas and the only reminders of this activity are the street names and ancient maps.

However, when talking about industrial activity and the spaces where it took place, we must not forget the Arsenale, the vast ship building yard of the Venetian Republic where "large galleys for voyages and slim

Patrician gardens, botanical gardens, fruit and vegetable gardens in convents and cloisters.

The Arsenale, the vast ship building yard of the Venetian Republic.

galleys for the fleet were built without interruption", i.e. this is where the fleet that the city owes its commercial success to was built.

Its origins are unclear: according to nineteenth-century tradition, it was founded in 1103 but this date has been disputed by present-day scholars. What is certain, however, is that in the fourteenth century the Arsenale was already a fundamental part of Venice and it continued to expand during the following centuries: in the fifteenth century it covered almost 14 hectares and by the end of the sixteenth century had reached approximately 26 hectares. It remained so until the fall of the Venetian Republic. It underwent numerous restorations, restructuring and expansion under the French, Austrians and during the period of the Kingdom of Italy in particular.

It remained fully functional until after World War II, was occupied by both the Military Marine and a Venetian shipbuilding company and covered 46 hectares. During the end of the last century naval activity gradually decreased and today parts of the Arsenale are used for cultural events of various kinds, such as art exhibitions and theatre performances.

When it was at its height, the Arsenale was home to cutting-edge shipbuilding yards, foundries where the two Moors with their bell were cast, now in the Clock Tower, weapon and gunpowder factories and warehouses, and timber warehouses. Just outside its walls were brick furnaces and ovens to bake rusks for the sailors; they made oars, sails, ropes ... everything an efficient fleet needed. We can only imagine the hum of activity in the area, when carpenters, blacksmiths, hemp dressers, caulkers and goodness knows how many others were working non-stop. When it was at the height of its activities, up to 16,000 people worked in the Arsenale!

14th century

16th century

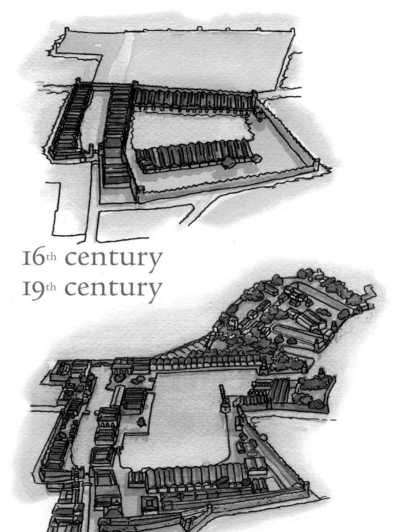

18th century

19th century

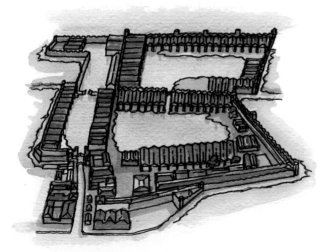

The most important work that revolutionised and upset Venice's status as an island was the railway bridge that crossed the lagoon, opened on 11 January 1846, thus finally marking the end of the city's splendid isolation

The city is no longer
an island

It was the evening of 11 May 1797: in the Great Council the elderly doge, Ludovico Manin, was voicing his fear and awareness that the end was nigh. The following morning, the Great Council assembled for the last time, with the declaration that the Republic had fallen. In Saint Mark's Square the people rebelled, raising the standard with the Lion to the cry of "Long Live Saint Mark". Obviously this made absolutely no difference and several days later, the French soldiers entered Venice. This was the first time such a thing had happened in the millenary history of the Venetian Republic. The dreams of the local Jacobins were shattered by foreign occupation, first the French, then the Austrians. The Republic had become so weak and fragile that it gave in and disappeared for ever. With the Campoformio treatise Venice fell under Austrian rule becoming a province of the Empire, which it remained for around seventy years, with the exception of the brief interlude when the French returned under Napoleon (1805-14). Before the city was handed over to the Austrians, countless works of art were plundered and the ships of the glorious fleet were either destroyed or sent to France. Venice was no longer a capital; the Veneto was united with Lombardy and Milan was the capital of Lombardy-Veneto. Over the decades, Venice was then subject to foreign rule – Austrian, French and then Austrian again – and this was accompanied by both considerable economic decline and modernisation.

Austria preferred the Port of Trieste, and as a result, the Venetian economy began its uninterrupted decline. The nobility found themselves having to sell their treasures to the highest bidder, *palazzi* fell into ruins, and the city visitors saw was fascinating, but one in disrepair: Venice was

With the Campoformio treatise Venice fell under Austrian rule becoming a province of the Empire.

just a memory of the glorious Venetian Republic. Ruskin, James and countless other famous writers lamented the city's decay, one that had been reduced to a "worn-out, commonplace shambles". Although the French remained for just a few years, they made considerable changes. They changed Saint Mark's Square, which had not been subject to such radical transformations for hundreds of years, by demolishing the Church of San Geminiano, built by the architect Sansovino, as well as five bays of the *Procuratie Vecchie*, to make room for the new Napoleonic Wing with its ballroom. This also marked the start of policies to create wide streets, which was to continue during the Italian period in particular, opening up *Via Eugenia*, which was later called *Via Garibaldi*, by filling in the *Rio di Castello*. This new thoroughfare then became the entrance to another of Napoleon's great works: the Public Gardens of Castello, which marked the beginning of the large works carried out to modernise the city. Indeed, the concept of public gardens was totally foreign to Venetians, both as a garden and public space, and actually originated in French town planning. This period also witnessed general urban renewal and maintenance with the expansion of the street network and the filling in of canals that were so small they were unhealthy. However, during all of these works, some attention was paid to the unique nature of Venice.
Once the French had left and Venice was part of the Empire, one of the fundamental guidelines of these nineteenth-century works, first by the Austrians and then by the Italians, was to modernise the city which meant making it as similar as possible to the other European cities, thus annulling the diversity and unique nature of which the city was so proud.

67

This marked the start of countless examples of the demolition of streets in the city, canals being filled in, and the creation of new, wider streets, thus radically transforming some of the historical characteristics of the city. One element was of particular importance. During the period of Austrian rule, more attention was paid to the pedestrian network than the canals, thus completely overturning life in the city, which had, until that moment, really been a city of water. The first measure taken to do so was the filling in of canals which, in the central area of the city in particular, was done with such great alacrity that in around 1840, someone finally began to worry, realising that they might be damaging the overall canal network. Under Austrian rule a total of 25 canals were filled in: *Rio dei Catecumen*i near *la Salute*, *della Carità* at the Accademia, *di San Leonardo* in Cannaregio, *degli Assassini* in San Marco, to name just a few.

The filling in of canals went hand in hand with the building of numerous new bridges to facilitate the pedestrian network; at the same time intensive restoration/rebuilding/extension was carried out on the existing bridges, as well as the construction of many new iron bridges, something totally new that can still be seen today in the city. These policies also foresaw the construction of a second bridge over the Grand Canal in 1852, the one mentioned earlier at the Accademia. This was then followed by the Scalzi Bridge, both of which differed considerably from the present-day ones: they were originally made of metal and were replaced in the twentieth century. The streets were obviously also improved and modified. The ideas and projects of that period were grandiose but very often they were never completed, either because of financial reasons or because of controversy regarding the best solutions, so that many proposals were blocked.

The policy of opening up wide streets began under the Austrians.

However, many streets were expanded, many itineraries simplified and straightened, while in the very heart of the city *Campo San Bortolomeo* was expanded, to give just one example.

The most important work to be carried out under the Austrians, the one that was to revolutionise and upset the insular character of the city, was the trans-lagoon railway bridge that opened on 11 January 1846, and thus marked the end of Venice's splendid isolation once and for all. Several years later, this led to the radical transformation of the area where the trains arrived when the Palladian Church of Santa Lucia was demolished to make room for the railway station.

In addition to these large-scale urban interventions, the architecture in the city was also subjected to countless restructuring, rebuilding and new buildings, all clearly visible in the city today. Thus, numerous buildings sprung up along *Riva degli Schiavoni* that were to be used as hotels, to meet the (new) vocation of Venice as a tourist destination. The same thing was to happen on the Lido a couple of decades later. Of considerable importance was the new building for the *Macello* [Slaughterhouse], located in the far west of the city, overlooking the northern lagoon, and which met the new hygienic-sanitary requirements of that period. Once the Austrians had left and Venice became part of a united Italy (1866), the local administrations undertook numerous initiatives to promote the city's development. These included several demolitions so that key pedestrian routes could be simplified: the *Strada Nuova, Bacino Orseolo* and *Via XXII Marzo*. The objective was to create a fluid pedestrian network between the most important areas of the city, and to do so, pre-existing buildings were demolished and replaced with new buildings.

70

Numerous works of demolition improved the pedestrian network.

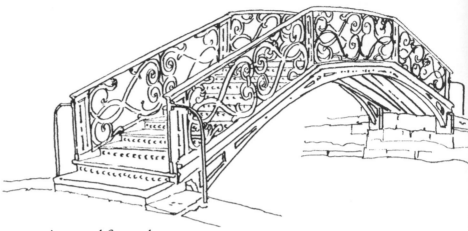

Strada Nuova was connected to prior Austrian interventions and formed a direct route between the Rialto and the Railway Station. *Bacino Orseolo* behind Saint Mark's Square marked the beginning of the axis Saint Mark's and San Luca, while also respecting sanitary requirements as the area was unhealthy and smelly. *Via XXII Marzo* linked Saint Mark's Square with the route towards *Campo Santo Stefano* (although it was never completed). These large-scale interventions were all accompanied by the construction of new buildings in the style of that period. One must also remember, however, that at times this modernisation process produced bizarre results. For example, along *Strada Nuova* the *palazzi* along the Grand Canal became the façades of the new street, although they were not usually of any particular apparent value; or a building was cut by the expansion of the street but was not demolished – a new façade was simply applied to the pre-existing building in the modern style.
Part of the modernisation of the city was its industrialisation.

The Commercial Maritime Station played a key role in this development, and was first established in 1870 on a vast area bordering the Zattere, most of which was artificial, i.e. obtained by the reclamation of the water area. The location of the Maritime went hand in hand with the construction of huge warehouses and radical intervention in the area behind, in Santa Marta, where the vast complex of the Olcese Cotton Mill and the Gas Works were built.

What took place on the island of the Giudecca during this industrialisation process is particularly interesting. Originally an island full of vegetable plots and gardens, with countless *casini* (gambling houses where the nobility would meet and have fun), with some small *palazzi*, numerous convents with cloisters and gardens, and dominated by Palladio's outstanding Church of the Redentore, during the nineteenth and twentieth century it was totally transformed into an industrial area.

75

Once the convents had been suppressed, vast areas became free and, while large gardens still remained on the side overlooking the lagoon, with the exception of the CNOMV ship building yards, in the other areas the following were built: Mulino Stucky, a beer factory, the factory of Fortuny fabrics, the so-called Vendramin warehouses and so on. The presence of these industrial activities resulted in the massive construction of working-class districts, which ended up transforming the island into a ghetto. However, during that period working-class districts were not only being created on the Giudecca: industrialisation made the construction of housing for the workers necessary, and this need, together with that for the redevelopment of several areas that were particularly unhealthy or in ruins, resulted in a series of "cheap, healthy social" housing complexes, with thousands of new apartments, starting from the end of the nineteenth century and in the first decade of the twentieth century. This work was either directly or indirectly managed by the City Council and before World War I, resulted in a total of more than 500,000 m³ of new homes, most of which were situated in the peripheral zones of the city.

Another important intervention was the construction of the aqueduct which, in 1884, marked the end of the ancient cistern system. Ever since then they have been closed and very often the ones inside the buildings have been covered and forgotten. There are a great number of them and they could, however, still play a role in our lives, helping us waste less water. However, this all took place more than one century ago. Ever since, the city has obviously continued to change, experiencing considerable growth, transformation and indispensable interventions regarding maintenance and restoration. It has also experienced a serious crisis:

Before World War I this work resulted in a total of more than 500,000 m³ of new homes, most of which were situated in the peripheral zones of the city.

its inhabitants are leaving the city and its population has been halved
during the last fifty years. The causes of this phenomenon
are complicated and this is not the right place to analyse them.
There is, however, one important problem that needs to be mentioned:
the high waters. The lagoon, the very origin of Venice and its source
of protection during its millenary history, which, in turn, the city has
protected by deviating rivers to avoid filling in and creating sea defences
– has created an emergence that is growing more and more serious:
the high tides that are flooding parts of the city with growing
frequency. The problem of the high tides has been the subject of debates
and studies and today great works are underway in an attempt to find
a solution by trying to control the tides to a certain extent.
There is another tide that is also threatening the city's fragile equilibrium:
the irresponsible tourism invading it, threatening both its identity and
survival.

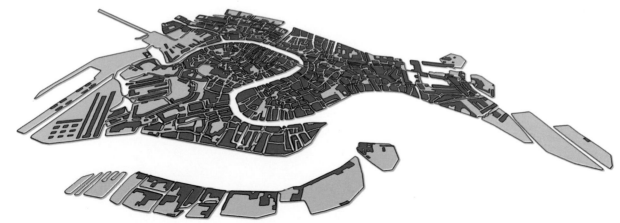

However, Venice is still a liveable place, with a rhythm of life that allows meetings and rest, but above all, it is one whose incalculable patrimony of beauty can help those who want to grow closer to the city, live better, even during the brief periods they visit.

Sixth edition
*Printed in September 2015
by Grafiche Veneziane, Venice*